GRAYSLAKE AREA PUBLIC LIBRARY

3 6109 00554 6392

P9-CPV-023

NO LONGER OWNED BY
GRAYSLAKE PUBLIC LIBRARY

EDGE BOOKS™

Video Games vs. Reality

SNEAKY SPIES

THE INSPIRING **TRUTH** BEHIND POPULAR STEALTH VIDEO GAMES

BY: THOMAS KINGSLEY TROUPE

GRAYSLAKE AREA PUBLIC LIBRARY
100 Library Lane
Grayslake, IL 60030

CAPSTONE PRESS
a capstone imprint

Y
794.8
TRO
1.19 dz

Edge Books are published by Capstone Press,
1710 Roe Crest Drive, North Mankato, Minnesota 56003
www.mycapstone.com

Copyright © 2019 by Capstone Press, a Capstone imprint. All rights reserved.
No part of this publication may be reproduced in whole or in part, or stored
in a retrieval system, or transmitted in any form or by any means, electronic,
mechanical, photocopying, recording, or otherwise, without written permission
of the publisher.

Library of Congress Cataloging-in-Publication Data
Names: Troupe, Thomas Kingsley, author.
Title: Sneaky spies : the inspiring truth behind popular stealth video game /
    by Thomas Kingsley Troupe.
Description: North Mankato, Minnesota : Capstone Press, 2019. |
    Series: Edge books. Video games vs. reality | Age 8–14.
Identifiers: LCCN 2018006073 (print) | LCCN 2018006701 (ebook) |
    ISBN 9781543525809 (eBook PDF) | ISBN 9781543525724 (hardcover) |
    ISBN 9781543525762 (paperback)
Subjects: LCSH: Espionage—Juvenile literature. | Spies—Juvenile literature. |
    Espionage—Computer games—Juvenile literature. | Spies—Computer
    games—Juvenile literature.
Classification: LCC UB270 (ebook) | LCC UB270 .T76 2019 (print) |
    DDC 793.9/20285—dc23
LC record available at https://lccn.loc.gov/2018006073

Editorial Credits
Aaron Sautter, editor; Kyle Grenz, designer; Tracy Cummins, media researcher;
    Tori Abraham, production specialist

Photo Credits
Alamy: Game Shots, 9, 27, GAUTIER Stephane/SAGAPHOTO.COM, 10; DVIDS:
Army photo/John Pennell, 21, U.S. Marine Corps photo by Lance Cpl. Steven Fox/
Released, 16; Getty Images: hphimagelibrary, 25, Jonathan Alcorn/Bloomberg,
23, PATRICK KOVARIK/AFP, 12, Photo Courtesy of Taser International, 24;
iStockphoto: decisiveimages, 4–5, GerMan101, 28, Krakozawr, 18–19; Library of
Congress: 13; Newscom: akg-images/Peter Connolly, 11; Shutterstock: CreativeCore,
Design Element, Dr Project, Design Element, Fotokvadrat, 8, frank_peters, Cover
Middle, Getmilitaryphotos, 7, Gorodenkoff, 20, 26, Jurie Maree, 17, Lukasz
Szwaj, Design Element, Sergey Nivens, 6, Serhiy Smirnov, Design Element,
silverkblackstock, Design Element, Zern Liew, Design Element; United States
Naval Special Warfare (SEAL): 14–15, chris.desmond@navy.mil, 22, U.S. Navy
photo by Mass Communication Specialist 2nd Class Martin L. Carey, 29

Printed and bound in the United States of America.
PA017

3 6109 00554 6392

TABLE OF CONTENTS

CHAPTER 1

Keeping It Quiet

It's the middle of the night when you enter the secure building. The lights are off and it's completely dark. But that's exactly what you want. With a trained hand, you tug your **infrared goggles** over your eyes. To you, the building looks fully lit. You walk silently past the guards in the dark. Before any of them can hear you, you've entered the computer room.

infrared goggles—special gear that shows the heat given off by people and objects as visible light

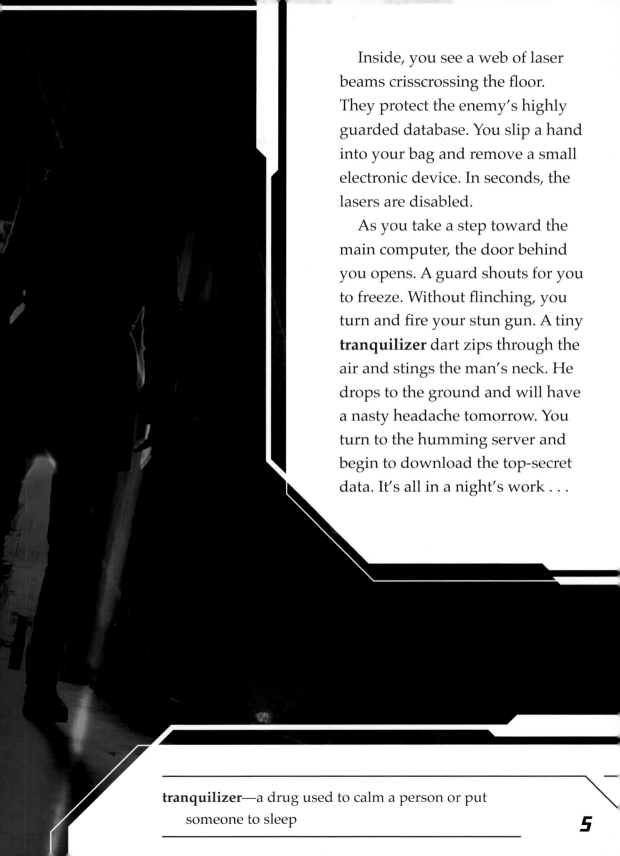

Inside, you see a web of laser beams crisscrossing the floor. They protect the enemy's highly guarded database. You slip a hand into your bag and remove a small electronic device. In seconds, the lasers are disabled.

As you take a step toward the main computer, the door behind you opens. A guard shouts for you to freeze. Without flinching, you turn and fire your stun gun. A tiny **tranquilizer** dart zips through the air and stings the man's neck. He drops to the ground and will have a nasty headache tomorrow. You turn to the humming server and begin to download the top-secret data. It's all in a night's work . . .

tranquilizer—a drug used to calm a person or put someone to sleep

Stealthy spies and secret missions have crept into the hearts of many video game fans. Gamers can become secret agents and spy on the enemy. Or they can be part of a secret military team to achieve an impossible mission. Few games can beat the rush of sneaking by your enemies to steal their top-secret plans.

stealthy—to move secretly and quietly

Military special forces teams are trained to carry out their missions without being discovered by the enemy.

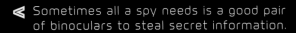

Video game developers look to real life to make games. They use real-life spy stories. They study spies' clothing, gadgets, weapons, and fighting styles. Game makers also research historical spies and secret missions to create goals for players.

Ready to beat the bad guys and save the world? Strap on your **night-vision goggles** and grab your gear. It's time to learn about the real-life events, history, and gear that inspire today's popular stealth games.

night-vision goggles—high-tech equipment that allows someone to see things in little to no light

CHAPTER 2

History's Secret Soldiers

Stealth-based video games involve moving quietly through the shadows and along rooftops. Many of these games require patience and perfect timing. These skills were used by secret organizations from the past.

Ninja Magic

In **medieval** Japan people feared ninjas. These spies sometimes wore dark clothing and snuck around in the dark. But usually they disguised themselves as regular people. Doing so allowed them to blend in to spy and collect information. Over time, people began to believe that ninjas had magical abilities. They thought ninjas could turn invisible, leap great distances, and even walk on water!

medieval—having to do with the period of history between AD 500 and 1450

In the game *Aragami*, gamers play a ninja-like warrior. Just like real ninjas, the game requires players to be stealthy. They must blend into each level's surroundings. Game designers also gave the main character legendary ninja powers. Aragami can turn invisible and **teleport** himself. He can even create dragons from the shadows to attack his enemies.

teleport—to transport oneself by instantly disappearing from one location and reappearing in another

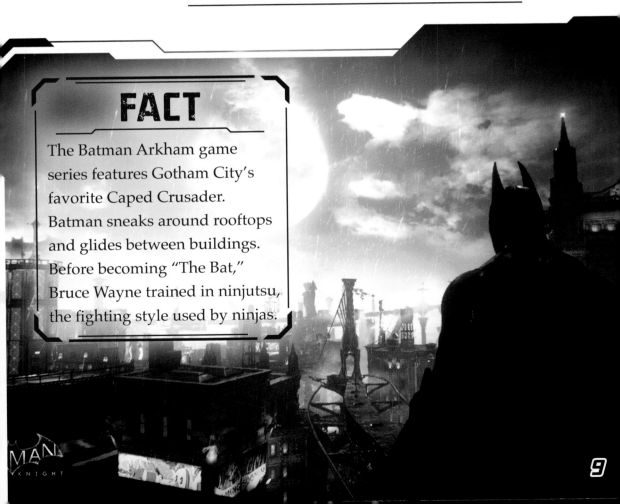

FACT

The Batman Arkham game series features Gotham City's favorite Caped Crusader. Batman sneaks around rooftops and glides between buildings. Before becoming "The Bat," Bruce Wayne trained in ninjutsu, the fighting style used by ninjas.

The Creed's Sneaky Deeds

Sneaky groups have been around long before ninjas. About 2,000 years ago the Romans controlled present-day Israel. A group of Jewish rebels called the Sicarii fought against the Romans. The Jewish **assassins** hid weapons inside their clothes. They quietly followed their Roman enemies through public places. Then they would kill their victims in surprise attacks and disappear into the crowd.

assassin—a person who murders a well-known or important person, such as a king or president

In the Assassin's Creed series, game designers draw inspiration from the Sicarii. Players are given hidden weapons and have amazing athletic skills. Gamers try to be as stealthy as the Sicarii. They blend into crowded places as they hunt their enemies. Just as the Sicarii fought against the Romans, the Assassins Order also fights for freedom. They work against the Templar Knights who wish to take control of the world.

FACT

The Sicarii were named after their weapon of choice, a curved dagger called a *sica*.

Silent But Deadly

Stealthy spies and agents aren't just found in the pages of history. Modern-day teams also work in the shadows. One famous but secret squad is the United States Navy's Seal Team 6. According to the U.S. government, the team doesn't officially exist. It instead operates under the name "Naval Special Warfare Development Group."

The team is often tasked with dangerous "can't fail" missions. Using high-tech gear, the team can sneak into an enemy camp at night. Once inside, the team silently carries out its mission and leaves before being noticed.

Game designers often look to military groups like Seal Team 6 to bring players the excitement of a high-risk mission. In *Rainbow Six: Siege* players work as part of a special team to shut down terrorist groups. Players use grappling hooks to **rappel** down walls and catch enemies by surprise. Like Seal Team 6, players need to be especially careful to get the job done quickly and quietly without getting caught.

FACT

The Rainbow Six series is based on the 1998 book written by late author Tom Clancy. The "Rainbow" unit is a fictional team inspired by real-life military squads and operations.

rappel—to slide down a strong rope

A Vengeful Spy

Fritz Joubert Duquesne was a South African man who fought against the British Army. During the Second Boer War (1899–1902), his family's farm was destroyed, his sister was killed, and his mother died in a concentration camp. Duquesne blamed Britain's Lord Herbert Kitchener for his tragic loss and vowed to get revenge. During World War I (1914–1919) Duquesne became a spy for Germany. In 1916 he signaled a German submarine to attack the HMS *Hampshire*. The ship was destroyed, killing Lord Kitchener and everyone else onboard.

CHAPTER 3

Tricky Tactics

In many stealth-based games, players use special **tactics** to reach their objectives. Sometimes they need to hide in plain sight. They may need to distract an enemy's attention. Or they may need to take out enemies quickly and quietly. Game designers look to real-life military training to give players a realistic game experience.

Moving into Position

Real-life snipers are trained to quietly sneak into the best position to shoot. This "stalk" training typically takes place in an open field. Snipers begin on one end of the field while the instructors are on the other. Students need to sneak toward the instructors without being seen. They move slowly and carefully. They usually need to crawl on their bellies inches at a time.

tactic—an action or plan used to achieve a goal

Λ Stealth tactics often include using camouflage to blend in with one's surroundings.

To be successful in the Splinter Cell series, players must learn the fine art of stealth. The game's main character, Sam Fisher, must move silently. He uses "stalk" methods like those of real military snipers. Fisher also crawls under obstacles and across large fields to complete his missions.

FACT

The game *Alien: Isolation* features a ferocious alien creature hunting humans aboard a spaceship. Players must learn to be patient and move slowly to avoid detection. Moving too quickly makes too much noise, alerting the creature to the player's location.

HALO Can You Go?

Sometimes the best way to carry out a mission is from the sky. In 1960 the U.S. Air Force developed the HALO technique for **paratroopers**. HALO stands for High **Altitude**, Low Opening. The soldiers secretly jump into battle from airplanes. Paratroopers free fall to a low altitude before opening their parachutes. This tactic makes it hard for enemy radar to find the soldiers. Using this technique, soldiers can reach the ground safely.

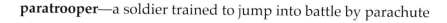

paratrooper—a soldier trained to jump into battle by parachute

altitude—the height of something above Earth's surface

The HALO jump method is a highlight of the game *Metal Gear Solid 3: Snake Eater.* The game's hero, Solid Snake, does a number of flips before diving to gain top speed. Like real HALO jumpers, Snake opens his parachute at the last moment to avoid enemy radar. Snake then begins his stealthy mission in the Soviet Union's thick forest below.

FACT

The HALO method is also used to drop supplies or vehicles to soldiers on the ground. This strategy helps make sure that enemy forces don't find the cargo.

Feeling Punchy?

Even the sneakiest of spies can be discovered. Sometimes there's little choice but to fight with one's fists. Police officers and soldiers are trained to use Close Quarters Combat, or CQC, to fight criminals. Many of the moves lock up the opponent's arms. The method prevents enemies from fighting back or firing a weapon.

Game makers often add CQC to their games. In game series like Splinter Cell and Hitman, players need to be ready to fight in hand-to-hand combat. Players can sometimes hide around a corner to grab opponents. Other times heroes can twist arms or kick legs out from under their enemies. But unlike in the real world, these moves often knock out the bad guys instantly.

FACT

CQC techniques continue to evolve as enemy tactics change. The hand-to-hand fighting methods use a variety of fighting styles, including martial arts, wrestling, and boxing.

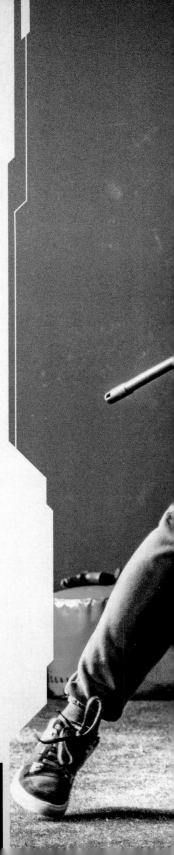

Krav Maga was developed by Israel's military forces. The self-defense martial art uses elements of boxing, judo, karate, and other fighting styles to disarm and defeat one's opponent.

CHAPTER 4

A Military forces use drones to safely find enemy positions and track their movements from a distance.

Great Gadgets

Being sneaky in stealth-based games requires more than walking on tiptoes. Using high-tech gear is half the fun. Some gadgets give the game's hero the upper hand. Others are designed to ruin the bad guys' day.

Jamming Out

Military drones are very useful for spying on an enemy's movements. These small aircraft are usually flown from the ground with a remote control. However, a gadget known as a "drone jammer" can make drones useless. A jammer floods an area with radio waves. The waves block signals from the remote control. The drone just hovers in one spot or falls from the sky.

The designers of *Rainbow Six: Siege* wanted to include this technology in their game. Players can use a signal jammer to keep drones away. The device can also stop remote-activated bombs from exploding. The jammer looks like a small griddle with four antennas attached to it. It looks odd, but it's useful for stopping the enemy from setting off bombs.

FACT

Signal jammers come in all shapes and sizes. Some look like internet routers or remote controls. Others look like rifles. They can be aimed to fire radio waves directly at a drone.

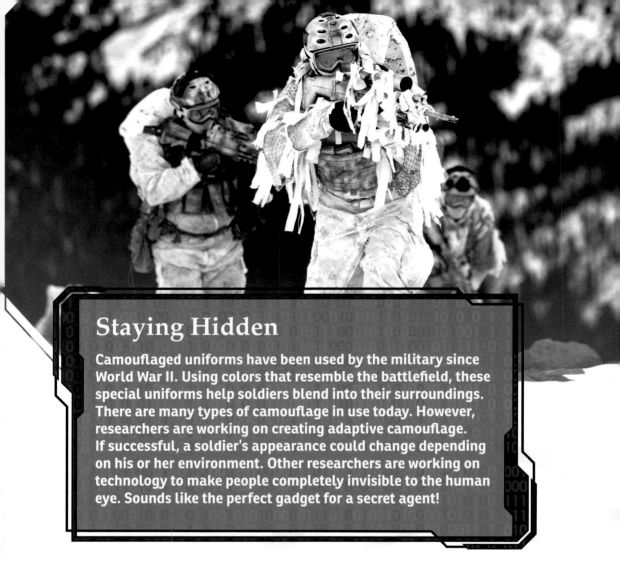

Staying Hidden

Camouflaged uniforms have been used by the military since World War II. Using colors that resemble the battlefield, these special uniforms help soldiers blend into their surroundings. There are many types of camouflage in use today. However, researchers are working on creating adaptive camouflage. If successful, a soldier's appearance could change depending on his or her environment. Other researchers are working on technology to make people completely invisible to the human eye. Sounds like the perfect gadget for a secret agent!

Don't Ogle the Goggles

Sneaking through the dark is the main tactic in many stealth missions. Night-vision goggles help spies and soldiers to find their way in the dark. Warm objects, including people, give off heat. Infrared goggles show that heat as infrared light. Warm objects look like glowing yellow and orange shapes in the dark. Other goggles increase the available dim light so users can clearly see their surroundings.

In *Splinter Cell: Blacklist* the game designers took night-vision goggles to the next level. Named the Fourth Echelon Goggles, players can use several different vision modes. Along with Night Vision, the goggles can use **Sonar** Vision. This mode allows a player to see enemies through walls, hidden land mines, and security cameras. These goggles don't exist in the real world. But they give players an exciting advantage over the enemy.

FACT

One of the strangest gadgets used in video games comes from the Metal Gear series. Whenever super soldier Snake needs to hide from enemies, he can simply produce a cardboard box and hide inside of it.

sonar—technology that uses sound waves to find objects; sonar stands for sound navigation and ranging

In the Splinter Cell series from Ubisoft, upgrades to the Fourth Echelon Goggles can even allow a player to detect people's footprints.

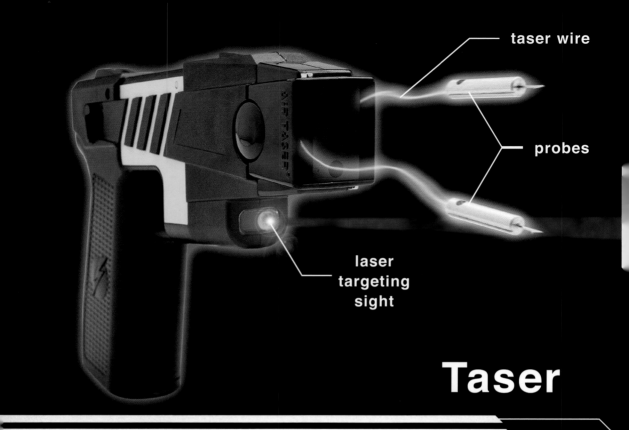

taser wire

probes

laser targeting sight

Taser

Non-Lethal Weaponry

Getting from Point A to Point B isn't always easy. Sometimes secret agents need to gently remove an enemy target to complete a mission. In some cases, players need to capture a human target unharmed.

In the real world, police and military forces often use Tasers to take down a suspect. These hand-held devices fire two small probes that attach to the target. Wires connected to the probes then deliver a painful electric shock. The jolt **paralyzes** the target and usually drops the victim to the ground.

paralyze—to cause the loss of the ability to control the muscles

Some games are designed to encourage players to use non-deadly force. *Metal Gear Solid: The Phantom Pain* is one example. Players are rewarded for using a tranquilizer gun instead of killing enemies. It shoots tranquilizer darts that put people to sleep. Unlike real-world Tasers, tranq darts instantly knock out targets in video games. The heroes can then hide the snoozing victims so nothing looks out of place.

FACT

Real tranquilizer guns are typically used on wild animals, not humans. The amount of drugs needed to knock a person out can vary by body size and mass. It's too dangerous to shoot a person with a tranquilizer gun. The end result could be a deadly overdose.

What the Hack?

Being a good spy often means stealing top-secret information. Researchers are working on devices that can remotely hack into enemies' secure computer systems. Devices that let spies secretly listen in on an enemy's phone calls are also in the works. Learning secret passwords and downloading classified data from afar would help keep secret agents out of harm's way.

▲ Secret agents often need expert computer hacking skills to steal enemy secrets or upload viruses to destroy enemy computer systems.

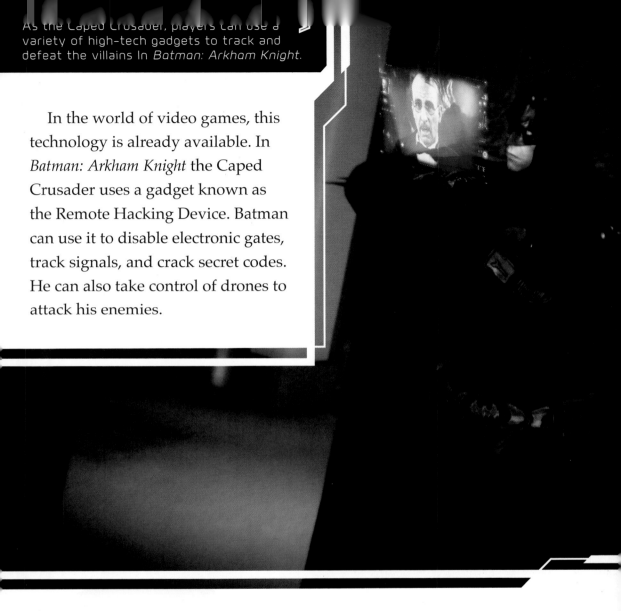

In the world of video games, this technology is already available. In *Batman: Arkham Knight* the Caped Crusader uses a gadget known as the Remote Hacking Device. Batman can use it to disable electronic gates, track signals, and crack secret codes. He can also take control of drones to attack his enemies.

FACT

One of the more useful items in Batman's Utility Belt is smoke pellets. When he's surrounded by thugs, Batman can smash one on the ground and escape in an instant cloud of smoke.

Shhh . . . Don't Make a Sound!

It's incredible to think that the most dangerous secret missions in video games are inspired by real life. Spy and stealth games include outrageous situations that would never happen in the real world. But game designers sneak in kernels of truth and real history into their stories. From secret agents and special forces teams to high-tech gadgets, real history has greatly inspired video game designers.

Fans of stealth-based video games enjoy becoming **virtual** heroes in the game world. Achieving a difficult mission and getting out undetected by the enemy can be a thrilling experience. Game makers know that basing games on real events and people adds a layer of realism that will keep players coming back for more.

virtual—not real; when something is made to seem real on a computer

GLOSSARY

altitude (AL-ti-tood)—the height of something above Earth's surface

assassin (uh-SA-suhn)—a person who murders a well-known or important person, such as a king or president

infrared goggles (in-fruh-RED GOG-uhls)—special gear that shows the heat given off by people and objects as visible light

medieval (mee-DEE-vuhl)—having to do with the period of history between AD 500 and 1450

night-vision goggles (NITE-vizsh-uhn GOG-uhls)—high-tech equipment that allows someone to see things in little to no light

paralyze (PAIR-uh-lize)—to cause the loss of the ability to control the muscles

paratrooper (PAIR-uh-troop-ur)—a soldier trained to jump into battle by parachute

rappel (ruh-PEL)—to slide down a strong rope

sonar (SOH-nar)—technology that uses sound waves to find objects; sonar stands for sound navigation and ranging

stealthy (STEL-thee)—to move secretly and quietly

tactic (TAK-tik)—an action or plan used to achieve a goal

teleport (TELL-uh-port)—to transport oneself by instantly disappearing from one location and reappearing in another

tranquilizer (TRANG-kwuh-lahy-zer)—a drug used to calm a person or put someone to sleep

virtual (VIR-choo-uhl)—not real; when something is made to seem real on a computer

READ MORE

Landau, Elaine. *Assassins, Traitors, and Spies.* Shockzone: Villains. Minneapolis: Lerner Publications Co., 2013.

Lusted, Marcia Amidon. *Ninja Science: Camouflage, Weapons, and Stealthy Attacks.* Warrior Science. North Mankato, Minn.: Capstone Press, 2017.

Price, Sean Stewart. *Modern Spies.* Classified. North Mankato, Minn.: Capstone Press, 2014.

INTERNET SITES

Use FactHound to find Internet sites related to this book.

Visit *www.facthound.com*

Just type in 9781543525724 and go.

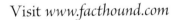

Check out projects, games and lots more at
www.capstonekids.com

INDEX

GRAYSLAKE AREA PUBLIC LIBRARY
100 Library Lane
Grayslake, IL 60030